ZEALOUS
MISSIONARY

ZEALOUS MISSIONARY

From the Perspective of
BLESSED FRANCIS XAVIER SEELOS

FR. RICHARD BOEVER, CSsR

Liguori

Imprimi Potest: Stephen T. Rehrauer, CSsR, Provincial
Denver Province, the Redemptorists

Published by Liguori Publications, Liguori, Missouri 63057
Liguori Publications, a nonprofit corporation, is an apostolate of the Redemptorists
(Redemptorists.com).
To order, visit Liguori.org or call 800-325-9521.

ISBN 978-0-7648-2857-7

Library of Congress Cataloging-in-Publication Data
Names: Boever, Richard A., author.
Title: Zealous missionary: from the perspective of blessed Francis Xavier Seelos / Richard
Boever, CSsR.
Identifiers: LCCN 2021020808 (print) | LCCN 2021020809 (ebook) | ISBN
    9780764828577 | ISBN 9780764872334 (epub)
Subjects: LCSH: Seelos, Francis Xavier, 1819–1867. |
    Redemptorists—Biography.
Classification: LCC BX4705.S517 B64 2021 (print) | LCC BX4705.S517
    (ebook) | DDC 266/.2092 [B]—dc23
LC record available at https://lccn.loc.gov/2021020808
LC ebook record available at https://lccn.loc.gov/2021020809

Printed in the United States of America
25 24 23 22 21 / 5 4 3 2 1
First Edition

CONTENTS

Introduction

AT MY BROTHER'S ISOLATED CATTLE FARM southwest of St. Louis, I often use a cabin as a hermitage. There, a wind chime rings. Aluminum tubes of varying lengths emit unique tones when they're struck by a wooden disk hanging in the middle. Most of the time when I look at the wind chime, I notice little more than the aluminum tubes. They are the chime's most evident features, but the heart of the instrument is the wooden disk in the center that makes them ring.

This chime makes me think of the lifelong accomplishments of Francis Xavier Seelos (1819–67), such as his selfless caring for yellow fever victims. On the wind chime (symbolizing Blessed Seelos' life), each tube represents a different achievement. To give purpose to the chime (his life) and make each tube sound sweet, it takes the heart of a saint and the wind of God.

In this book, my intention is to help you know Blessed

Francis Xavier Seelos as a person and acquaint you with his accomplishments. Having studied Francis Xavier's life and letters, I wrote this biography in the first person. While I have taken poetic license and some liberties, this book is historically sound, reading much like the excerpts of his letters that you will find throughout the text. Some of Fr. Seelos' quotations have been highlighted in display type. For more of Fr. Seelos' letters, I recommend you read the collection gathered in *Sincerely, Seelos* by Fr. Carl W. Hoegerl, CSsR.

My book includes the date of each letter and the person to whom Blessed Seelos wrote. I pray that my efforts inspire you and provide you insight.

Fr. Rich Boever, CSsR

Chronology

1819	Born, Füssen, Germany (January 11)
1825–31	Elementary school
1828	Confirmation
1830	First holy Communion
1831-32	Private academic tutoring
1832–39	*Gymnasium*, Augsburg, St. Stephan's
1839–41	University, Munich, philosophy
1841–42	University, Munich, theology;
	Dillingen seminary, St. Jerome
1843	Sails to America (March 17–April 20)
1843–44	Novitiate at St. James, Baltimore
1844	Professes vows as a Redemptorist (May 16)

1844	Ordained a priest (December 22)
1845–54	Parish priest, St. Philomena, Pittsburgh
1847	Novice master, St. Philomena
1851–54	Pastor and religious superior, St. Philomena
1854–57	Pastor and religious superior, St. Alphonsus, Baltimore
1857–62	Pastor, superior, prefect of students, Sts. Peter and Paul, Cumberland, MD
1862–65	Students move with Seelos to St. Mary's, Annapolis, MD
	Pastor and religious superior
1863–65	Superior of mission band, Annapolis
1865–66	St. Mary's, Detroit
1866–67	St. Mary's Assumption, New Orleans
1867	Dies of yellow fever caring for the sick, New Orleans (October 4)
2000	Beatified by St. John Paul II

A List of Illustrations and Photographs

Page 14: The Benedictine Monastery of St. Mang, Füssen, Germany: Francis Xavier Seelos was baptized and confirmed, received his first Communion, and was an altar server at St. Mang's Church.

Page 17: Francis began his formal education at age six in this building, once known as "the old *kornhaus.*"

Page 20: The Seelos family moved to this house on Sankt Mang Platz after Francis' father became sacristan of nearby St. Mang's Church.

Page 22: Francis continued his schooling by taking secondary classes at St. Stephan's *gymnasium* in Augsburg.

Page 26: Francis entered Royal Ludwig Maximilian University in Munich as a philosophy student, where he learned skills expected of a Bavarian gentleman, including dancing and fencing.

Page 32: Soon after his acceptance into the Redemptorists as a novice, Francis bid farewell to the only life he had known and booked passage on the *Saint Nicholas* to the United States.

Page 42: During his assignment to St. Philomena in Pittsburgh, Fr. Seelos felt he learned what it really meant to be a priest.

Page 44: Fr. John Neumann was pastor and rector of St. Philomena when Fr. Seelos joined that community. They became close friends. Fr. Neumann was later canonized as a saint.

Page 51: This document, dated June 15, 1848, records Fr. Seelos' petition to become a United States citizen.

Page 52: Fr. Seelos became a United States citizen on October 6, 1852, this document shows.

Page 54: Fr. Seelos became pastor of St. Alphonsus Parish in Baltimore in 1854. This major responsibility included supervising seven parish priests and eight religious Brothers.

Page 62: The Civil War raged nearby while Fr. Seelos was pastor, community superior, and director of students at Sts. Peter and Paul in Cumberland, Maryland. Formation students playing sports once were mistaken for enemy agents and temporarily detained at gunpoint.

Page 70: Fr. Seelos was overjoyed with his 1862 appointment to St. Mary's in Annapolis, Maryland. He was especially thrilled by the brand-new Gothic church with its excellent organ.

Page 76: The mission cross of Fr. Francis Xavier Seelos

Page 81: Saint Mary's Church, Detroit

Page 82: Fr. Seelos was laid to rest at St. Mary's Assumption Church in New Orleans beneath a statue of Our Mother of Sorrows that he had blessed as a parish priest.

Page 89: This carved marble slab marks Fr. Seelos' grave at St. Mary's Assumption Church. His relics are now interred in a reliquary at the National Shrine of Blessed Francis Xavier Seelos in New Orleans.

Page 90: Portrait of Blessed Francis Xavier Seelos painted by Giuseppe Antonio Lomuscio, an Italian artist.

Page 98: Portrait painted by Giuseppe Antonio Lomuscio

Page 102: A present-day view of the National Shrine of Blessed Francis Xavier Seelos

The Benedictine Monastery of St. Mang, Füssen, Germany: Francis Xavier Seelos was baptized and confirmed, received his first Communion, and was an altar server at St. Mang's Church.

CHAPTER 1

European Years

FÜSSEN IS A KIND OF FAIRY-TALE TOWN nestled near the Bavarian Alps in the shadow of King Ludwig's Hohenschwangau Castle in southern Germany. In my day, the still-young nineteenth century, we were only about 190 households with 1,547 inhabitants, and all but twenty residents were Catholic. The capital, Munich, is about sixty miles northeast of our little town, but in those days we didn't go that far from home. We were small-town people who greeted each other with *"Grüss Gott!"* meaning, "May God bless you!" It was wonderful living among the gabled roofs, narrow streets, and rolling hills that surrounded the town.

I was born at home, Number 13 Spitalgasse Street, on January 11, 1819, and brought to church to be baptized that same day. I would be granted only forty-eight years of life. I was the sixth child born to the Seelos family. Elizabeth was first; followed by the twins, who died during their first year on earth; then Josephine and Ambrose. After me, more children: Antonia, Frances, Ulrich (who lived but a short time), Anna, Adam, and Kunigunda. Twelve children were given to my parents: three entered into the holy state of matrimony, three remained single, and two became religious sisters. I became a Redemptorist priest who missioned in North America.

My father, Mang Seelos, was a weaver and cloth maker by trade, and my mother, Frances Schwarzenbach, was a holy *hausfrau* who raised the children. I was rather sickly as a child, which gave my mother an extra challenge. My brothers and sisters would say I was also a bit spoiled. Probably true. They noted that I liked to laugh, for which I sometimes got into trouble at school. I enjoyed my friends and liked to cut up a bit. One day when I was in grade school, I used my father's tailcoat and hat to dress up as a clown for the day's carnival festivities. When Father saw me, I got into trouble.

Each day the family rose early for Mass, followed by breakfast and our other daily routines. Before each meal, we prayed together, and after dinner in the evenings the children took turns reading aloud about the saint of the day. On one occasion, when it was my turn to read, I mispronounced the name of St. Polycarp as "Saint Polycrap." My brothers and sisters laughed wildly, but my father corrected me sternly, and I learned how important it was to pronounce the words I read the right way. His admonition came in handy later in life during my preaching. There's no doubt we were raised in a very Catholic manner, and we thought that was the way every family lived.

Francis began his formal education at age six in this building, once known as "the old kornhaus.*"*

When I was six years old, I began my formal education in the *volksschule*, generally thought of as our parish school but officially a public elementary school. The school building was located on the corner of Schrannengasse and Brunnengasse. It was known in town as "the old *kornhaus*" because the first floor was the marketplace for the sale of corn to the local inhabitants. The school occupied the second floor. Our school year comprised two semesters, from November to Easter and from May through August. Classes were held six days a week, from eight until ten o'clock in the morning and from one to three o'clock in the afternoon. We were drilled in what is called "the three R's" in America. We also had classes in religion and moral development, and we attended morning Mass each day.

I especially liked music and singing, and I even learned the violin. Music delighted me and helped me express all the wonder I felt within my heart. I went to the volksschule for six years and was rewarded with good grades for my studiousness. I was also an altar server at St. Mang's Church, where I received my confirmation in 1828 and first Communion in 1830. These were special celebrations for me and happy days.

When I was a child, the Industrial Revolution was sweeping across Europe, and life was changing for many people. Technology affected my father's trade because new machines could manufacture cloth cheaper than he could weave it. We suffered financially during my elementary school years. My parents never shared their worries about money with us children, but we understood that their lives were difficult. Then, in 1830, unexpectedly and by God's providence, my father got a new job. He was appointed the sacristan at St. Mang's Church, and shortly after my sister Kunigunda's birth, we moved into the sacristan's house on Sankt Mang Platz.

> Letter to the family in 1862: But believe me, dear sister, growing up this way is just the best, where children get a bit acquainted with poverty in this world, and get to know what need is, and how parents have to worry to obtain their daily bread. Such children understand very well that this world cannot be the ultimate goal of our desires; and that there must be a higher and better life, for which the present one is only a sorrowful preparation. If children learned this, they have learned a great lesson which, together with later sorrows, has brought many a frivolous young person back again to the right path. So, dear sister, strive to thank God for everything; to be patient in suffering, and in this way to offer yourself for your family.

The Seelos family moved to this house on Sankt Mang Platz after Francis' father became sacristan of nearby St. Mang's Church.

Our new house was a great improvement as our family home. It was adjacent to the church which held such a special place in my family's life. My father certainly merited the new position, for he was very pious and had an excellent reputation among the townsfolk. In our new home, one of the benefits of Father's new job, we had much more space for my brothers and sisters and their activities. Personally

I loved living so close to the church, where I could help my father. I am certain the location helped deepen in me the spirit of faith and prayer we experienced at home.

When I was twelve years old, my time at the local elementary school ended. This presented me with a fork in the road. I was expected either to be apprenticed in some trade or continue to a more formal education at the secondary school, or *gymnasium*, at St. Stephan's. For us in Bavaria, the gymnasium was not a place one went for exercise, but it was the next step in the education process between elementary school and university. Unfortunately, progressing to higher education also entailed significant expense. That influenced the educational choice for many of my classmates and me. My family did not have the money necessary to continue my education, even though I did very well in elementary school. However, the parish priest at St. Mang's, Fr. Xavier Anton Heim, came to my rescue. He was convinced I should continue my education and committed himself to provide me with money for meals and an allowance while I was at the gymnasium. Therefore, I was able to begin the next step of my schooling at St. Stephan's in Augsburg, ninety miles north of my hometown of Füssen. Until I was able to enter the gymnasium at the start of the next school year, Fr. Heim instructed me privately. His work with me enabled me to go directly into the second year at St. Stephan's when I was thirteen years old.

Francis continued his schooling by taking secondary classes at St. Stephan's gymnasium in Augsburg.

CHAPTER 2

Setting Out on My Own

BEING THIRTEEN YEARS OLD IS A CHALLENG-ING TIME for any young man, and I was no exception. My schoolmates and I were giving serious attention to what our future life would look like and the steps needed to reach our intended destinations. We were excited about growing into adulthood, but that goal remained in the far distance. For me, setting forth into a new, unfamiliar environment at the end of my elementary school years would entail cutting the family's apron strings. However difficult, this was the time to move to the next part of my life, so I left for St. Stephan's. There were several boys from Füssen going to the same school, including two of my cousins. Their familiar faces made the move somewhat easier for me.

Augsburg was fifteen times larger than my hometown of Füssen, and only half the population was Catholic. The city was known as the place where the Augsburg Confession, the primary confession of faith of the Lutheran Church, was formulated. The environment there seemed so different, and it frightened me more than a bit. I was heartsick to trade the warmth of my family, home, and town for a student rooming house.

The *Stephansplatz*, where St. Stephan's formed three sides of the quadrangle, had only existed for four years as an independent school before I entered, but already there were 600 students registered. The school offered an eight-year course of study. Since I entered during the second year of the Latin School, this became my home for seven years. We studied Latin, Greek, German, religion, history, and geography, and we were expected to attend Mass daily plus Sunday afternoon vespers. My first semester consisted of twenty-two hours of classes each week: twelve of Latin, four of German, and two hours each of geography, arithmetic, and religion. I also took a class in French. In spite of being very busy, I did well in my grades. All my years of study included this kind of intense curriculum, but I was able to manage.

Music still stirred my soul. I improved on the violin and enthusiastically played the instrument at Mass. One Sunday, I continued playing after the song had concluded. As a result, I was told I was no longer needed as an accompanist. I also loved to sing—so much so that a friend had to ask me not to sing so loudly in church.

Because of the intensity of my studies, I delighted in returning home for vacation each year. This was a time for hiking through the beautiful Bavarian valleys and mountains. On one occasion, I hiked into the Austrian Tyrol and all the way to Switzerland. Sometimes my father hiked with me. During one of our excursions, we walked 150 miles to Einsiedeln Abbey in Switzerland. Whether in study or on vacation, my heart was always filled with joy. What a blessing! Others seemed to sense this and enjoyed my company, which further delighted me.

During my years at St. Stephan's, I thought more and more about becoming a priest. I envisioned becoming a cleric in my home diocese, with my sisters living in the household as cook and housekeeper, a practice common in those days.

On August 26, 1839, I won the approval of the examiners of St. Stephan's, which qualified me to continue my education at university. I was twenty-two years old. Like secondary school, university was expensive, and my family had no extra funds. To continue my education, I would have to win a scholarship. A petition for this was drawn up and signed by the mayor of Füssen and other officials and sent to the provincial council. By the grace of God, the petition was approved, paving the way for me to move on to higher education. I was going to the Royal Ludwig Maximilian University in Munich.

Francis entered Royal Ludwig Maximilian University in Munich as a philosophy student, where he learned skills expected of a Bavarian gentleman, including dancing and fencing.

CHAPTER 3

To Munich
for University

WHEN I ENTERED my next phase of study in Munich, the year was 1839. The Royal Ludwig Maximilian University had a long history, dating back to 1472. Within the university were five schools: theology, philosophy, law, medicine, and political economy. I began in the school of philosophy and roomed on the fourth floor of an apartment house at 20 Karlsplatz. I donned the colorful outfit of a university philosophy student, complete with spurs and a bright red cap, and joined the student activity group, where I learned the arts of dancing and fencing—skills expected of any young gentleman of Bavaria.

One time I recall returning to Füssen on vacation dressed in my uniform of a philosophy student. "What's the matter with you?" my mother exclaimed. "I do not know you anymore." I told her that I was now a philosophy student at the university, and this was what we wore. That was not to be for her. She said I was still the same boy she raised and I should take off the uniform for simpler clothing.

I was uncertain about my vocation when I entered university, and the thought of priesthood weighed on my mind. After two years, I completed my studies in philosophy and continued in the school of theology, not as a seminarian but as a regular student. The theology curriculum entailed three years of intense study, with thirty hours of classes each week. I did well in my studies, but at the same time never forgot to laugh, sing, and play my violin. However, all was not smooth sailing.

In February of my third year of university studies, I contracted smallpox. It struck me ruthlessly. All of the symptoms were present: fever, fatigue, sweating, chills, headache, and weakness in my legs and arms. Eventually I had to be carried to the hospital for a two-week stay. In my fevered hallucinations, I felt that I was visited by my family members, one after another, which was a consolation for me. Naturally I fell behind in my studies. When I recovered, I diligently pushed myself to catch up with my schoolwork. After completing my first-year theology studies, I made a choice that would change the course of my remaining life. I finally settled into a decision so long in coming—to prepare for ordination to the priesthood.

Letter to my brother, Adam, about my decision, November 28, 1842: It is therefore God's holy will that I go to that country which I already showed you on the map during those happy hours when we were always together on Sunday morning....If it were up to me alone, I would always stay with you and our family, but I will not and cannot resist the inner call that comes from the other side, but I will give myself freely with entire love.

In 1842, I applied to the Redemptorists of North America for acceptance into their Congregation as a clerical student, but mail across the Atlantic was very slow. Two of my Augsburg classmates, Max Leimgruber and Thaddeus Anwander, had already joined the Redemptorist novitiate in Switzerland to prepare for ministry in the United States. Two diocesan priests I knew from Augsburg, Albert Schaeffler and Joseph Mueller, had also entered the Redemptorists' formation program. Local Catholic newspapers gave a great amount of space to the work of German emigrant priests doing marvelous ministry overseas. All of these things made a strong impression on me. As the beginning of my second year in theology school approached, I knew I wanted to be ordained a priest and live as a Redemptorist in the United States. Still, I had not yet received a reply to my application to the American Redemptorists, so I entered

St. Jerome's in Dillingen as a seminarian for the Diocese of Augsburg. I would not be a student there long. Shortly after arriving at Dillingen, word arrived from America that the Redemptorists would accept me as a candidate to join them in the ministry in North America.

I donned the colorful outfit of a university philosophy student, complete with spurs and a bright red cap, and joined the student activity group, where I learned the arts of dancing and fencing—skills expected of any young gentleman of Bavaria.

Soon after his acceptance into the Redemptorists as a novice, Francis bid farewell to the only life he had known and booked passage on the Saint Nicholas *to the United States.*

CHAPTER 4

Saying Goodbye, Sailing to America

AS I BEGAN MY SECOND YEAR of theological study at the university—but before I knew I would be accepted into the Redemptorists—I returned home for what could be my final visit. It was disheartening because I realized that soon I might be leaving my family, never to return to Füssen. I told them I intended to enter the seminary to prepare for ordination to the priesthood. My family was delighted with my decision to enter the seminary. As was the custom in Bavaria, my sisters started thinking about living with me in the rectory after ordination as cook and housekeeper. I hadn't yet told them that I didn't plan to remain in Bavaria. When they discovered this, they would certainly be disappointed. It was only after I was accepted into the Redemptorists that I told the family the news of my leaving Bavaria. I had previously spoken to my father about becoming a missionary, so he anticipated my decision. But to spare the others pain, we did not speak of this with them on this final trip home. When I left, the embraces of my family were emotional and heartfelt. My father, who already realized I wanted to be a missionary in America, sent me forth with his finger pointing upward, meaning that the next time we would see each other would be in heaven.

On the feast day of St. Cecilia in 1842—November 22—I received a reply about joining the Redemptorists. Fr. Alexander, the superior of the Redemptorists in America, wrote: "The undersigned superior of the Congregation of the Most Holy Redeemer in the United States declares that the theologian, Mr. Francis Xavier Seelos, beloved in the Lord, has been received among the members of this Congregation and for this purpose has been summoned to Baltimore." I was overjoyed. From that day on, I especially cherished the annual feast of St. Cecilia.

After I finally heard from the American Redemptorists, I didn't return to the university as a student. I went to Augsburg on December 9, 1842, where I lived in the rectory of Fr. Heim while I prepared for the journey. I needed a passport and dimissorial letters from the Augsburg Diocese so I could eventually be ordained overseas. I received my passport December 27, 1842. It described me as "six feet tall, slim, hair and eyes of brown, nose thick, mouth large, chin rounded." I was twenty-four years old. After attending to the legalities of travel, I moved on to the Redemptorist house in Altötting, ninety-three kilometers from Munich, until I could make final arrangements for travel to Baltimore. In the 1840s, approximately one and a half million immigrants arrived in the United States, mostly German or Irish. Since a high percentage were Catholic, the Church in the United States was strained. The need for German-speaking priests was monumental. I believed I could serve the faithful in this new environment and dedicate my life to their care. Their faith served the immigrants as a reassuring anchor in a strange, new world.

In Altötting, I was to join the American superior and three other men who were also entering the Redemptorist Congregation in America. We would be sailing on the ship *Saint Nicholas* out of Le Havre, France, on the feast of St. Patrick, March 17, 1843. The ship carried 141 passengers and took five weeks to cross the Atlantic Ocean.

Letter home just before sailing, March 17, 1843: In a few hours, I will depart from Europe....Our ship is called the *Saint Nicholas*. I have waited to the last minute to write to you. Time is running out....The weather is very favorable. At ten o'clock, we have to be aboard ship, and now it is already three-quarters to. It is a wonderfully beautiful and brand-new American packet ship. Farewell to all, Father and dear Mother, and dear brothers and sisters. Many greetings to all our relatives and acquaintances, especially to the reverend pastor. Many greetings. *Adieu.* Farewell, farewell, until further news. In prayer let us meet in the Sacred Hearts of Jesus and Mary. Farewell to all.

My father, who already realized I wanted to be a missionary in America, sent me forth with his finger pointing upward, meaning that the next time we would see each other would be in heaven.

CHAPTER 5

Beginning My American Ministry

FEW BEFORE ME HAD MADE THE LONG VOYAGE to join the Redemptorist community and serve the German-speaking Catholics in America. For example, three priests and three Brothers had come to the United States from the Redemptorists eleven years earlier, but a permanent settlement that could support a community of priests and religious Brothers still was not to be found in the Midwest.

Originally the missionaries envisioned working among the native peoples, but eventually discovered that, as one man wrote, "for every Indian who was converted, ten Germans lost the faith." The need to serve immigrants was immense, and since they also came from Germany, the priests and Brothers were equipped to serve them. After seven years going from place to place, the community accepted work among the German immigrants in Pittsburgh. By the time I arrived in America, the number of confreres had increased to ten priests and five Brothers, with houses in five cities. Fourteen new members came to the United States with me to join the American Redemptorists in 1843: six priests, five Brothers, one professed clerical student, and two novices—including myself.

We anchored in New York Harbor after a long journey across the Atlantic and then traveled to the parish of St. James in Baltimore for our initiation. When I stepped off the ship onto solid land, I knew I had left behind my life in Europe, but I still did not yet know what lay ahead of me in America. I was, however, confident that this was what God wanted me to do, and I praised him with the groaning of a heart that would miss my past but was filled with anticipation for all that was to come. I began my novitiate on May 16, 1843, and prepared for my vows, which I professed a year later. After novitiate, I continued my theological studies at St. James until my ordination to the priesthood on December 22, 1844. I served as assistant parish priest at St. James for eight months, delivering my first sermon in April 1845. One of the priests criticized my delivery rather harshly! In addition to my parish duties, I also served the religious sisters in the local convents with Mass, confessions, and conferences.

Letter home from Baltimore, August 1, 1845: Here, God especially gave me a longing in my inmost being to offer myself, to give myself to him completely; a desire that, with the grace of God, is ever increasing, and still leaves the wish: "Oh, if only I could give more; if only I could give now what I formerly misused." This desire to bring a sacrifice to God again and again extends to everything that I ever loved in this life, and upon which my heart was set. And so, when I think of home, my ever-remembered parents and brothers and sisters, and the people who are dear to me, I offer them all up to God and recommend them to his love, and desire only that all of us will meet again in heaven. And you should not have any worries about my temporal needs. I receive everything that a tender mother would want to give her son.

During my time in Baltimore, I was told to study English. I was not pleased to study the new language, but I obeyed. We spoke German in our community, and there was plenty of apostolic work among the German immigrants. Eventually I was able to get by in English, but it took a long time before I found any comfort in speaking it.

Letter about English to his sister, Sister Damiana, 1864: On and on I must now give conferences and sermons in English; and even at table and in going about, I hear no other language. And that is no small penance, because I cannot ever get to like this language. It is so strange that it almost makes one's mouth and tongue sore. English is certainly not the language of the angels, but for the valley of tears and the place of exile it is good enough.

We were also instructed to wear secular clothing on the street because of a terrible anti-Catholic prejudice among some Americans. Some of the longtime residents considered themselves and their families more "truly American" because they had been here longer than the newly arrived immigrants, many of whom were Catholic. Because of their antagonism, it seemed best not to draw attention to ourselves as priests and religious.

I did, indeed, experience a cultural shock in my new environment. Nonetheless, I was healthy and wanted for nothing. We had heat in the winter, water in the house, and I felt accepted and supported in the community. This was important to me because, in these early days of ministry, I felt very backward and seemed to make a thousand mistakes every day. I certainly had an adjustment period in my new American life.

Fragment of a letter home, December 14, 1844: Everything, the bedbugs, the insects, the religious sects, the language, and so many things more, as the vulgar spirit of speculation, business, and money, the coldness and dryness of the people—nowhere a cross or a church of pilgrimage—no happy faces, no songs, no singing, everything dead. See, all these things were completely against my nature. But precisely the joyful acceptance of them, in God's boundless grace, made so clear to me in the mystery of the renunciation and patience in this world that I feel that I am much too fortunate in the possession my religious confreres and all the spiritual and temporal blessings that are bound together with it.

I wasn't long in my assignment in Baltimore. In August 1845, I was transferred to the St. Philomena community in Pittsburgh. Though I entered my ministry in Baltimore, it was in Pittsburgh where I really learned what it meant to be a priest.

ST. PHILOMENA'S CHURCH.
PITTSBURGH, PENN.

*During his assignment to St. Philomena in Pittsburgh, Fr. Seelos felt
he learned what it really meant to be a priest.*

CHAPTER 6

Pittsburgh—
St. Philomena, 1845

THE CITY OF PITTSBURGH was filled with immigrants from Scotland, England, Ireland, and Germany. They labored in the ironworks and foundries or in the coal mines along the river. Though these workers were vital to the economy, they were not well accepted by many of the city's wealthier residents. We Redemptorists lived among the German immigrants in an area known as Bayardstown. The parish was referred to as "the factory church" because the place had been a cotton factory before being used as a church. Eventually the parish was named for St. Philomena, and a grand building program was begun to prepare a worthy place of worship for the congregation.

Fr. John Neumann was pastor and rector of St. Philomena when Fr. Seelos joined that community. They became close friends. Fr. Neumann was later canonized as a saint.

When I arrived in Pittsburgh in 1845, the parish pastor and rector of the community was Fr. John Neumann (1811–60), who would be canonized as St. John Neumann in 1977. I was quick to appreciate his goodness. He directed me as a spiritual guide and confessor. He cared for all my needs, body and soul, and loved me as his own son. I knew him a bit from my days at St. James in Baltimore, but in Pittsburgh I came to know him much better. We shared the same room with only a curtain separating our places of rest. I often heard him praying late into the night. He was a remarkable person with whom to live.

We were active in our ministry. I celebrated 150 marriages and 370 baptisms in just two years. This was in addition to the daily Masses, the many hours of confessions, and the individual spiritual direction I gave to parishioners.

Even though we endured constant financial struggles, on October 4, 1846, a new church was dedicated. The effort to build the beautiful St. Philomena's, along with countless pastoral activities, exhausted all of us. But the toll was especially noticeable with my dear confrere, John Neumann. One day a member of the community saw him spitting blood and referred the issue to our superior in Baltimore. To our dismay, but also knowing it was necessary, Fr. Neumann was transferred to Baltimore to rest. In reality, I don't think it was much of a rest because two months later he was appointed superior of all the Redemptorists in North

America! Fr. Joseph Mueller succeeded Fr. Neumann as pastor, and I continued as assistant pastor.

Our community ministry extended much farther than just the parish in the city. We served the German immigrants as far west as Steubenville, Ohio, and as far east as Wheeling, West Virginia. New duties were added to my responsibilities when, after only three years in vows as a Redemptorist, I was appointed novice master by Fr. Neumann. I was surprised. I was only twenty-eight years old, but he must have trusted me. On my annual retreat, I prayed that I could win over the hearts of the novices and make them open only to devout conversation that inflamed the heart. As for me personally, I wanted to feel the chill and dampness of winter. I embraced such hardships with joy. The floor would be my bed. I would put no salt or other spices on any of my food. *Xavier,* I told myself, *you must be transfigured and consecrated through fasting and prayer. Then you will be strong.*

> Letter home to family, 1845: Time, in which we have found nothing to offer up to God, is lost for eternity. If it is only the duties of our vocation that we fulfill with dedication to the will of God; if it is the sweat of our faces that, in resignation, we wipe from our brow without murmuring; if it is suffering, temptations, difficulties with our fel-

lowmen—everything we can present to God as an offering and can, through them, become like Jesus his Son. Where the sacrifice is great and manifold, there, in the same proportion, is the hope of glory more deeply and more securely grounded in the heart of him who makes it, etc.

My assignment as novice master lasted only sixteen months, during which I had four clerical students and three Brother candidates. It was a short assignment because the new vice provincial of the Redemptorists in North America believed the novices needed to be prepared for vows in Baltimore, where they would be closer to the Congregation's authorities. That meant they had to move to St. Alphonsus Parish. But my direction of novices did not end when the Redemptorist novices moved from Pittsburgh. Six Sisters of Mercy arrived in Pittsburgh from Ireland—the first of these incredible women to serve in the United States. I prepared seven of their novices for their profession of vows.

When I was thirty-two years old, a change of administration took place at St. Philomena's. I was appointed pastor of the parish and rector of the community. My ministry didn't change dramatically. I still served the faithful as a priest, but now I was also the one who had to see to the overall well-being of the parish facilities.

One of my first concerns in my new position of authority was to establish a place for orphaned German children. We had the practice of presenting orphaned children for adoption from the pulpit at Sunday Masses, and worthy families often took them into their homes. However, more assistance was needed, especially for the littlest ones. We established our orphanage in 1851 and, by the grace of God, the marvelous School Sisters of Notre Dame took charge of the orphanage. What a blessing!

Part of a pastor's job is raising the necessary funds to keep the parish going. We needed a new organ chamber, new gutters, and interior renovations to the church. All of this costs money! I found that raising money entailed much effort and sweat, and the funds did not flow unless one did a lot of complaining and constantly made a big noise. This wasn't in my nature, and I didn't like doing it. Nonetheless, it was necessary, so I learned to do it.

I officially became a United States citizen during my time in Pittsburgh. In those days, an immigrant could apply for citizenship after he or she had lived in the United States for five years, had no record of civil offense, and renounced allegiance to the country from which he or she emigrated. I met those qualifications and, on October 6, 1852, received my naturalization papers, which finalized my citizenship process.

During my days in Pittsburgh, two of my family members died in Bavaria. My sister, Kunigunda, who was only twenty years old, fell from the hayloft and died almost instantly. Then, my father, Mang, died on September 11, 1853. I didn't learn of these deaths for some time because of the slow mail delivery between Europe and the United States. Strangely, however, I dreamed of my father very near the day of his death. In my dream, he was uncommonly handsome.

> Letter to my mother, November 1853: When I read the way our dear father died, so beautifully and so resigned, I have the consoling trust that in the other world, he will have a very honorable place, and that now he is in a position to obtain for all of us every great grace. Dearest Mother, be firm, because every member of the family that God takes out of your heart is a most beautiful sacrifice when you remain resigned to the most holy will of God. See, dear Mother, that's how one becomes holy. To be sure, our hearts will sometimes bleed and cry out with pain; but it is precisely God Himself who heals the wound far more beautifully.

In Pittsburgh there were many opportunities to practice the virtue of praying for the sick. God often blessed sick parishioners with recovery when I prayed with them.

I praised God for his mercy but felt worried because some people jumped to the conclusion that the cures came from my hands. I knew healing was always a gift from God. Also, when faced with those who did not have enough, I often found that I could do with less. Once, I gave my boots to a poor man who had tattered shoes. Another time I gave my mittens to a washerwoman on a bitter-cold day. I found so many opportunities to be charitable.

Pittsburgh always held a special place in my heart. Though I stayed at St. James in Baltimore for a bit of time after my ordination, I consider St. Philomena as my first genuine assignment. I served there from 1845 until 1854. During those years, I was assistant pastor, novice master, and eventually pastor of the parish and rector of the community. It was in Pittsburgh that I learned how to be a priest. I was young and zealous. I recall that on one occasion Fr. Neumann chided me for my enthusiasm and told me that we have to leave God, the Lord, something to do! I hold dear the men with whom I was stationed and the good souls of the parishioners. I would take the knowledge gained in Pittsburgh into all my future assignments.

This document, dated June 15, 1848, records Fr. Seelos' petition to become a United States citizen.

Fr. Seelos became a United States citizen on October 6, 1852, this document shows.

I gave my boots to a poor man
who had tattered shoes.
Another time I gave my mittens
to a washerwoman
on a bitter-cold day. I found
so many opportunities
to be charitable.

Fr. Seelos became pastor of St. Alphonsus Parish in Baltimore in 1854. This major responsibility included supervising seven parish priests and eight religious Brothers.

CHAPTER 7

Baltimore— St. Alphonsus, 1854

IN JANUARY 1854, FR. GEORGE RULAND was named provincial of the American Province. At that time, I was transferred from Pittsburgh to St. Alphonsus Parish in Baltimore to succeed him as pastor and superior. I was also named second consultor to the provincial, arriving in Baltimore for my new assignments on March 2. The Redemptorist community of St. Alphonsus also served both the parishes of St. James and St. Michael in the city, as well as many German-speaking immigrant communities in a far-flung territory. It was a daunting job. The congregation in each church was large, and all of the priests were kept busy with the sacraments, spiritual conferences, the needs of the religious in each neighborhood, and providing spiritual direction to the parishioners. But there also were endless administrative details to manage for each parish.

We were very involved in religious education; the school at St. Alphonsus alone had 1,300 students. In 1856, we recorded 1,098 baptisms in the parish books. These were immense tasks, but we were pleased to be able to tend to the spiritual needs of so many souls. God certainly showed his presence in our parish communities. When I first arrived at St. Alphonsus, there were seven other parish priests and eight Brothers stationed in the community, and we all worked diligently.

Later in 1854, the confreres gathered at St. Alphonsus to elect delegates for the general chapter of the Redemptorists to be held in Rome the following year. At that meeting, important decisions would be made for the Congregation worldwide, and delegates from every unit were elected to decide these issues. I was secretly hoping to be elected to that general chapter, not because of any personal pride to be elected to such an important meeting but because it would have provided an opportunity to visit my family in Bavaria while I was in Europe. I knew that was somewhat selfish, but it was the truth. To my disappointment, I was not elected. Our administrative structure for the Congregation in America consisted of a provincial, the vicar, and myself as the second consultor to the provincial. When Fr. Ruland, the provincial, departed for Rome, Fr. Gabriel Rumpler, the provincial vicar stationed in Annapolis, Maryland, assumed authority in the United States. I got the role of second-in-charge of the American confreres since I held the position of second consultor. I remained in Baltimore, where I continued as pastor, superior of the community, and as the second consultor.

On May 30, 1855, I was informed that Fr. Rumpler, who was also my superior, had suffered a mental breakdown. As second consultor, I was next in line to take charge. This was a serious issue, and I had to journey to Annapolis to handle the situation. At first, I suggested that Fr. Rumpler take a rest, but he refused. As his behavior had become increasingly erratic, it became necessary for him to be moved to Mount Hope, an institution run by the Sisters of Charity for the mentally ill. Life in such an institution was unpleasant; I could see that immediately. I visited him two weeks later, and it appeared that his condition had improved greatly. But I was wrong. It was a burden to my heart to have a confrere confined to an institution so, possibly against the advice of the Mount Hope staff, I brought him home with me to St. Alphonsus. He then requested to return back to his assignment in Annapolis, so I brought him back to his home. Things did not work out well. Fr. Rumpler had to be readmitted to Mount Hope Hospital.

My compassion for Fr. Rumpler was frowned upon by some confreres. Sixteen letters were sent to the higher authorities in Rome disapproving of what I thought were acts of kindness to the sick man. Some confreres were furious with me for my empathy, which they judged as misguided. In turn, the letter-writing to the superiors in Rome offended me and I felt betrayed. I was wrong to bring Fr. Rumpler back to community—this was proven by his having to be readmitted to Mount Hope—but the reactions of some confreres hurt me.

I found that dealing with a suffering confrere to be so heart-moving, especially when I could not help him. One's suffering always touched me deeply. I felt I had not handled things well with Fr. Rumpler when I brought him home from Mount Hope and pondered my softheartedness. I concluded that I was not rigid enough to be in authority when difficult decisions must be made. In November, I fell on my knees before the provincial superior and confessed that I was unqualified for the job of superior of the community. In the end, things fell into place and, despite my perceived weakness, I was reappointed superior and pastor of St. Alphonsus in Baltimore but was relieved of my office as second consultor.

The devotion of the people toward me was an affirmation for me, especially in troubled times. I returned to Allegheny to minister in a parish mission. Allegheny is actually a part of Pittsburgh, just across the Allegheny River, and my former parishioners received me with such affection!

Letter home, early 1855: It was eleven months since my departure (from Pittsburgh). O what jubilation there was when Father Seelos came back again! Many people kept on praying to have this blessing once more, as they called it. Most of them could not say a single word and merely greeted me with tears. They knelt down on the street to receive my blessing. Only with difficulty could I prevent some from kissing my feet. There was such a crowd around the confessional that once they forced the door off its hinges. In short, I was very much embarrassed and upset that the people had such a good opinion of me, that everyone has the wrong impression of me.

During my assignment in Baltimore, I was delighted that we were able to institute the beautiful devotion known as Forty Hours. With the Blessed Sacrament exposed on our altar, people came with great devotion. This was done at St. James Church. We decorated the entire sanctuary of the church with a Turkish red drape, hired the best musicians, and had devotions all day long. I was in my glory and felt so encouraged by the piety of the parishioners and by my own time of personal prayer. The Forty Hours devotion was so well received! I considered this renewal a great blessing. The devotion continued for many years afterward.

During my time in Baltimore, several wonderful healings took place when I prayed for the sick. I prefer not to discuss them for fear of taking credit myself instead of placing it where it belonged—in the compassion of God. I knew I was an instrument of God, but I also knew we are all called to be his instrument. In fact, I noted weaknesses in myself.

In March 1857, I fell sick. After hearing confessions for many hours, when I left the confessional, I stretched to restore my circulation. Blood started coming from my mouth. One of the confreres saw this and reported the incident to the provincial. From Saturday afternoon until Sunday afternoon, the blood continued issuing from a hemorrhage in my throat. Even so, I returned to the confessional after supper on Saturday evening and again Sunday morning. I had to stay in bed for several weeks and would eventually be transferred to St. Mary's Parish in Annapolis for health reasons.

Letter to Miss Mary, 1855: My yoke is sweet and my burden light!—That is not the yoke itself, but the manner in which we receive it, when near us, when pressing on our shoulder. Only the manner in which we act in such moments sweetens the cross of our vocation daily—knowing that sanctification and glorification of our humiliated flesh indispensably requires the fire of tribulation, requires a generous mind to undergo them, the meekness of a Lamb and the strength of a Lion in order to submit, to persevere.

In Annapolis, I was reappointed novice master. There were fifteen clerical novices who would eventually be ordained priests and ten novice Brothers. But this assignment in Annapolis would be short-lived. I would be reassigned there years later but, on this round, after only a month I was sent west to Cumberland, Maryland. I was appointed to be the prefect of our professed students who studied there. The former director of students was considered too rigid, melancholic, and ignorant of the American character. I was seen as the person who could bring stability to the house of formation.

The Civil War raged nearby while Fr. Seelos was pastor, community superior, and director of students at Sts. Peter and Paul in Cumberland, Maryland. Formation students playing sports once were mistaken for enemy agents and temporarily detained at gunpoint.

CHAPTER 8

Cumberland, Maryland—
Sts. Peter and Paul, 1857

I WAS TRANSFERRED TO CUMBERLAND in 1857 to replace the director of our professed students. It was decided that a change was badly needed, so I traveled 140 miles west of Baltimore, to Sts. Peter and Paul Parish.

Cumberland had two Catholic parishes: St. Patrick's for English speakers and Sts. Peter and Paul for German speakers. The city, nestled in the Allegheny Mountains, was known at the time as the gateway to the West. There were 6,000 inhabitants, and the city served as a transportation hub for the B&O Railroad and for barge traffic on the Chesapeake and Ohio Canal. It was predominantly a Protestant town where Redemptorists in 1849 established a permanent outpost after previously serving the area's German immigrants out of Baltimore.

A poem by Francis Xavier Seelos, 1856:

In God alone I seek for rest,
For nothing else can make me blest.
In secret sighs to him I moan,
And refuge seek in God alone.

In God alone, I hope to live,
He all his gifts does freely give;
My heart and soul let Him now own
Die nature, sense; live God alone.

And, then my Soul, what canst thou wish
Besides this object of thy bliss?
Thy sins confess, thy frailties own,
and strive to live for God alone.

On May 18, I was appointed pastor of the parish, superior of the community, and director of students. When I first arrived, there were 300 parishioners, and the community numbered three priests and eight Brothers. It was a relatively small parish then, but there were also forty-two professed Redemptorists in studies preparing for ordination to the priesthood. Luckily the confreres in the parish were zealous, competent men who skillfully performed so many of the parish duties. Of course, I took my part in the parochial responsibilities. Both the activities of the parish and the number of parishioners grew rapidly. We celebrated all the major feasts of the Church with great solemnity and inaugurated the Forty Hours devotion.

Not all of the happenings, however, were delightful for me. I was disappointed that, during Easter week of 1858, I had to summon the students to the common room and tell them that Fr. Isaac Hecker and four other Redemptorists were dispensed from their vows. This was difficult news for me to communicate to young religious who were still in discernment about their own futures. Some of those who were dispensed would eventually form a new Congregation—the Paulists. They felt called to minister more directly to the American culture and in the English language. They were skillful preachers, and I was hopeful their new direction would be blessed. It was, however, trying for me to see them leave the Redemptorists, and I was unhappy about it. I had to summon my hope that this was God's plan for them, and I hoped their ministry prospered among the English-speaking people of the United States.

Life went on for us at Sts. Peter and Paul's Parish. In August 1858, Archbishop Francis Kenrick consecrated the new parish church and, the next day, administered confirmation to 102 confirmands.

I was invited to return to St. Alphonsus in Baltimore in 1859 to celebrate Christmas in my former parish and to preach at the dedication of the new St. Michael's Church the day after Christmas. It was so good to see so many of the parishioners who received me with great graciousness and tenderness. Of course, when I returned to Cumberland, I once again immediately dove into my duties as pastor, rector, and director of students. Our community numbers grew each year so that by 1860 we numbered three priests, sixty students, six professed Brothers, and six novice Brothers.

One disagreeable situation during my Cumberland years was the startling news I heard, by way of rumor, that the bishop of Pittsburgh, Michael O'Connor, had submitted his resignation to Rome for health reasons and had recommended me as first on his list of candidates as his replacement. I wrote to everyone I could think of, begging them to pray that this not become a reality. I even wrote to the Holy Father, telling him I would be a poor choice. Luckily the pope had sent a cardinal to speak with our superior general in Rome about my qualifications. The superior general reported that I would not be a good choice because I was not a good manager of temporal affairs, and that the American and Irish clergy would not like a bishop of German descent in Pittsburgh.

While continuing my apostolic work both as parish

priest and formation director—and even in the midst of the rumor about being ordained a bishop—my primary concern was that I personally stay on the straight and narrow way of Jesus. I set my course of action based on my beliefs in how God works in our lives. I sincerely prayed not to be appointed bishop of Pittsburgh but knew I must be open to God's plans. I expressed my deepest beliefs in a letter to two of my sisters, both nuns. When I found out that I was not chosen to be the bishop, I was greatly relieved and hosted a party with the students that lasted an entire day to celebrate the fact. I was so relieved that God didn't invest me with a miter.

The students and I got along quite well. They were very open to formation and diligently applied themselves to the task. We also knew how to enjoy excursions into the countryside together. I found that such informal times were very productive for their formation, and I enjoyed these trips as well. Indeed, there were formal lectures about religious life. I continued to teach some of the theology classes and occasionally had to give a correction or two, but formation, in my opinion, went beyond this. Life experience is a great teacher! But sometimes the focus was so much on daily life that the work of salvation was neglected.

Letter to my sister, Antonia, from Cumberland, 1862: Dear Sister, in conclusion, I must tell you about a few strange things in America. We not only have a sewing machine and a washing machine, but also a machine with which the Brother cook in the kitchen peels potatoes. I almost always have to laugh when I see it; it goes so fast. In the rooms we usually use tallow candles, but in the refectory, in the corridors, and in the church (but not at the altars) we use gas for lighting. The windows are made in such a way that they stay put when they are opened, and you can close them again without difficulty. The lamps are made in such a way that you don't have to push up the candle as it burns, which often is quite difficult, but you press and push the lamp together and more of the candle comes up. On the trains, there is water in the cars, where everyone can get a drink, and in summer it is even cooled with ice. And there are toilets in the cars, all enclosed. They discover everything for comfort, but not for the salvation of their souls, these poor Americans.

Cumberland is close to the southern border of Maryland, next to Virginia, a state that was part of the Confederacy during the Civil War. One time, our students were playing some sport on the hillside. In the furor of war, nerves were often frayed. A young man from town saw the students playing sports in the field and ran to town shouting that enemy troops were seen at Sts. Peter and Paul. A panic ensued and, at gunpoint, the students were rounded up. Luckily, after allowing the locals to go through the house to guarantee that we were not enemy agents storing weapons of war, all ended peacefully. It was a frightening day. Again, this illustrates my point: formation is never separate from the realities that surround the men being formed.

After five years at Cumberland, the student formation program for professed members of the Congregation was moved to Annapolis, while the novitiate was moved to Cumberland. It was believed that the frigid winters and muggy summers in Cumberland were not conducive to good health, and while students could endure a one-year novitiate in a harsh climate, the longer formation time for the professed students should take place in a more pleasant climate. We were all transferred to Annapolis.

Fr. Seelos was overjoyed with his 1862 appointment to St. Mary's in Annapolis, Maryland. He was especially thrilled by the brand-new Gothic church with its excellent organ.

CHAPTER 9

Annapolis, Maryland— St. Mary's, 1862

I WAS SECRETLY PLEASED WHEN I HEARD of my appointment to Annapolis in 1862. The community had been elevated in importance to a rectorate, an ecclesiastical honor for the St. Mary's parish. Along with caring for our students, I was appointed the rector in charge of the community and parish pastor. As such, I saw to the needs of all the confreres at St. Mary's. I still taught sacred Scripture and gave conferences and lectures about religious life as a Redemptorist to the assembled group. I also had regular individual colloquia, or informal meetings, with each student to discuss his progress in the Redemptorist life we were called to live.

Letter to my sister, Antonia, 1862: Annapolis is now so wonderful that it really is too beautiful for me. A brand-new Gothic church, unusually lovely, with an excellent organ! The house is uncommonly big and built only since my last departure from there. It has eighty rooms, and my whole family will be seventy strong. Do renew your prayers for me that I will be up to this responsible job. It is very important.

For myself, I continued to practice mortification. I tried to practice the virtues recommended by the Redemptorist Rule for each month. I urged our students to be disciplined as well. If we believed that all suffering and misfortune is sent to us from God for our sanctification, then every hardship is also a blessing.

While I was at Annapolis, the Civil War continued to rage. A military draft was begun in March 1863 for males ages twenty through forty-five. As such, the thirty-six students and I were eligible for the draft. We decided to ordain twenty of the students immediately because there would be less chance of them being drafted as priests than as students. Still, the draft worried me. One could avoid the draft by paying three hundred dollars, but we did not have that kind of money. I decided I must go to the city of Washington to speak with President Lincoln. I went there in July with

Fr. Adrian Van de Braak. President Lincoln was gracious to me during my visit, and though he wouldn't issue a special protection from the draft for our men, he assured me our situation would resolve itself satisfactorily. None of us were drafted. He invited me to return for another visit after the war was concluded. This, unfortunately, never happened.

> Letter to Miss Mary, August 2, 1863: Thirty-six of our students, besides myself, are in danger of being selected for military service. For this reason, another priest and I went to Father Abraham. He treated me kindly, but [Edwin] Stanton (the Secretary of War)! If the feast of rough characters should ever be celebrated in the Church, Stanton will get an octave added.

In December, I was called to Fortress Monroe to minister to the soldiers injured in the war. This fortress at the southern tip of the Virginia peninsula guarded Chesapeake Bay. I went there twice from Baltimore by steamer. I was able to celebrate Mass and hear confessions afterward. An Irish Catholic man gave me supper and then I returned to the chapel to hear more confessions until midnight. My visit continued the following day with a trip to the hospital, which had fifty beds. The men at Fortress Monroe were filled with gratitude for my visit. I returned to Annapolis on December 10.

Letter to my brother, Ambrose, December 1862:
All were filled with tears, and often the words
were repeated that the appreciative soldiers ad-
dressed to me in gratitude: "God bless you!" This
was necessary because I couldn't expect any money because for many months now they had not
received any pay. I was richly repaid by the fine at-
titude of the soldiers, most of whom had not been
to confession for three or four years. For many it
was even longer, and with several, twenty years.

After I returned to Annapolis, I discovered that not
all of the confreres were happy with the way I exercised
my office as prefect of students. In May 1862, Fr. Joseph
Mueller had been the novice master in Annapolis and I had
been the prefect of students in Cumberland. The decision
made by the provincial government to exchange the places
of formation by sending the novices to Cumberland and to
bring the professed students to Annapolis with me as prefect displeased Fr. Mueller. As time went on, he developed
an antagonism toward me. He wrote to the superior general
in Rome. I was denounced because I allowed the students
to play music and to study even during their free time. He
didn't approve that I gave them ready access to the library
and secular journals, and that I even allowed them to stage
a play, which required two weeks of practice before the

performance. Rome listened to Fr. Mueller's complaints. Without consulting the local superiors, on September 13, 1862, a stricter man from Holland, Fr. Gerard Dielemanns, was appointed prefect. I had served three terms as prefect of students and the new appointment was quite unexpected by me. Even so, I was relieved to surrender the burden of being prefect to another man. I officially remained at St. Mary's as pastor and rector for another year but dedicated myself more fully to the ministry of preaching parish missions.

My letter to the superior general, Rome, December 1862: Fr. Dielemanns is already in our midst as prefect. The whole change went forward without any difficulty, because all were happy to see it as the greatest of blessings and accepted the new prefect with gratitude. I personally feel myself equally obligated in gratitude to Your Paternity, because you freed me from this difficult and responsible office. I will be happy to go hand in hand with the new prefect and to help him whenever he may wish my help.

The mission cross of Fr. Francis Xavier Seelos

CHAPTER 10

Life as a Home Missionary, 1863

I HAD SERVED IN PARISHES since my ordination, and during that time had many occasions to preach parish missions and retreats. I knew well the power of parish missions and was pleased to be assigned to this ministry full time. In fact, I liked this apostolate more than any other assignment because the ministry was directly related to preaching the gospel and didn't require constant administrative duties. Missions touched the faithful so deeply! Of course, while being a parish missionary, I also continued to give retreats to priests and religious.

Letter to my sister, Antonia, 1862: Last summer, our fathers gave missions in the State of Iowa (pronounced "eiwaa") along the Mississippi River. Here the fathers had much to suffer, principally the terrible heat and the tiny churches which, besides, were full to suffocation. The temperature was 105 degrees in the shade and sometimes even higher. And then these settlements were of mixed nationalities, made up of some who could only understand English and of others who only understood German, so that all sermons and instructions had to be given twice, which, together with hearing many confessions, even into the depths of the night, is extremely...exhausting. But our loving God seems to want such exertions from the missionaries to bless their labors all the more. For this reason, the fruits of these missions were very exceptional. Not only Catholics were completely renewed, but also many of the Protestants were converted.

The parish missions comprised sermons and spiritual exercises for the purpose of renewing and strengthening the spiritual life of the faithful and for the conversion of lapsed Catholics. Normally the mission in a particular parish lasted one or two weeks. Even though I was the superior of the mission, I did not often assign myself to deliver "the great sermon" in the evening because my English was not as flowing as my fellow missionaries. I spent my time hearing confessions and leading the spiritual exercises.

I preached missions in Missouri, Illinois, Wisconsin, Michigan, Ohio, Pennsylvania, New York, New Jersey, Connecticut, and Rhode Island. In those years the esteem of the local pastors for the Redemptorist missionaries continued to grow, so much so that in 1865, the provincial declared that he could not accept twenty-five requests for missions because missionaries were unavailable for the work. I was able to devote myself to this work for several years, often amazed at how God blessed the efforts we missionaries made.

Letter to my sister, Antonia, and family, 1862: But it is self-evident that the effects of the mission are not due to us but to the blessings that come from above. This becomes more and more evident when you consider that I and my companions were just about exhausted from six months of hard work...even our minds were gone. Even with the greatest effort, we could hardly get out a few words and had lost our appetite for food. Still, the less we could do, the more did our loving God and his dear Mother Mary do.

After a few years of preaching missions, I went to St. Mary's Parish in Detroit for a brief assignment. I was delighted by that assignment because, for the first time in many years, I could simply be a parish priest without authority. I quickly returned to the ministry of being a parish priest. My time in Detroit, however, was fleeting. In August 1866, I was sent to New Orleans.

I preached missions in Missouri, Illinois, Wisconsin, Michigan, Ohio, Pennsylvania, New York, New Jersey, Connecticut, and Rhode Island. In those years the esteem of the local pastors for the Redemptorist missionaries continued to grow.

Saint Mary's Church, Detroit

Fr. Seelos was laid to rest at St. Mary's Assumption Church in New Orleans beneath a statue of Our Mother of Sorrows that he had blessed as a parish priest.

CHAPTER 11

New Orleans—
St. Mary's Assumption, 1866

I ARRIVED IN NEW ORLEANS ON SEPTEMBER 28, 1866. On the train ride with me to the Crescent City, one of its nicknames, there was a School Sister of Notre Dame also traveling there for her apostolic work. She asked how long I would be staying. I replied that I'd be in New Orleans for a year and then die.

In my day, New Orleans was not an assignment most Redemptorists thought of as a plum one. It was hot and humid, with so many deaths from fevers that most preferred not to be assigned there. I, however, was very pleased to be going there. There were seven priests and six Brothers in the local community that served three churches: St. Alphonsus for the English-speaking, St. Mary's for the German-speaking, and Notre Dame for the French-speaking. Fr.

John Duffy was the rector of the community and pastor of all of these parishes. Nonetheless, other priests were given special charge of each of the parishes. I told the rector that it was good to be assigned to the sunny South as an ordinary soldier without authority. I did not get off the hook so easily; I was appointed prefect of St. Mary's Church and was expected to make most of the decisions for the parish with Fr. Duffy's approval. With the assistance of other priests and Brothers of the community, I was responsible for the apostolic work in the parish. In addition, I was appointed prefect of the Brothers and spiritual director to the German-speaking School Sisters of Notre Dame. My regular duties included celebrating Mass, hearing confessions, visiting the sick and orphans, and preaching and giving conferences to various religious communities in the city. There was always much to do, and I was fully engaged in being a parish priest.

> Letter to Timothy Enright, CSsR, Christmas Day, 1866: Oh, what a blessed winter as that in New Orleans—I had no idea, though you often told me. And the Southern plants!!! The bananas, oh, wisdom of God! Oh, beauty of that creative power which brought to existence such vegetation. Sometimes it happens to me as to the Queen of Saba, "and she had no breath any more" for admiration.

During my stay in New Orleans, I gathered, without intent, a large following of faithful sons and daughters. I spent long hours in the confessional, never rushing any of them. I promised to always receive each penitent with gentleness and strove to live up to that promise. I also was the first person to respond to sick calls in the homes of our parishioners—especially at night so the other priests could rest.

I had only been in the parish two months when, on my name's day, December 3 (the feast of St. Francis Xavier), there was such an outpouring of affection for me that I was caught off guard. I always found it easier to celebrate the outpouring of love toward others than to receive such an outpouring toward me without embarrassment. There was in the parish a society of about 200 women, mostly old and poor, that some of the priests affectionately referred to as the "Old Beauties." They worked hard to make my feast day a special time. I was sometimes teased by the confreres for being too nice to them. I responded that rudeness does no good and kindness can do no harm. If a priest is rough with people, he injures himself and others. He sins in his rudeness against charity, patience, poverty, humility, and self-denial. He scandalizes all who witness his actions. He turns away souls by the hundred, not only from himself, but also from God and religion. As you can surmise, I felt strongly about this point of view.

The apostolic work at St. Mary's was intense, and I tried to handle as much of the ministry as I could. I found people were always ready to respond to me in this effort and were very grateful. Of course, the tasks were not limited to St. Mary's alone. I also did as much as I could in the English-speaking parish of St. Alphonsus and the French-speaking parish of Notre Dame. My English still had a German accent and, though I could completely understand others speaking to me in English and French, I sometimes had difficulty expressing myself as clearly as I wished in those languages. But the people didn't appear to hold my imperfections against me. The people of God are very gracious.

As time went on, the horrors of yellow fever continued to ravage the parishes. Nonetheless, we were never reluctant to go into the homes of the sick, administer the sacraments, and bring them the consolation we could. In those days, we thought the fever was transmitted by personal contact, not understanding that it was the result of a bite from a certain mosquito that was plentiful in the city. In 1867, the fever was also present in our community. Some of the confreres, because their sicknesses, were taken out of their usual rotations. This added to the responsibilities of those priests who remained healthy to bring the balm of the Church to the homes of parishioners. On some days, the men were so busy that we didn't see each other, even though we lived in the same rectory.

On September 17, 1867, I contracted the fever. Eventually the rector ordered me to bed. I would not arise from the sickness. Normally the fever abated after nine days. I slept much during this period. Unfortunately, the fever did not pass. I grew ever weaker and eventually received the last rites. The confreres were continually at my bedside praying for me. They surprised me with their affection, often crying as they saw my struggles. The newspaper even began to give an account of my progress or lack thereof.

I went through all the horrors of the disease and was embarrassed by not being able to care for myself. I knew I would die. I told the community how blessed it was to die in the Congregation of the Most Holy Redeemer. I urged them all to value their vocation. I apologized to them for my shortcomings and inadequacies. Finally, on Friday, October 4, at 5:50 in the evening, I passed from this life to everlasting life. I was laid out that evening and all night in the church, then buried the next day beneath the statue of Our Mother of Sorrows, which I had blessed while I was active in the parish.

A poem, 1863:

O day surely singular in all of earthly life;
You alone still the holy yearning of pure souls;
You give courage to say an eternal farewell to the
    world,
When God has given an invitation for a beautiful
    sacrifice:
Immediately to stay only in the peaceful house
    of God,
And to strive only for the exalted virtue of the
    angels.
O eternally sweet day of joy!
Day of jubilation desired by the soul:
On you alone is my gaze always fixed,
On you alone is found all my joy.

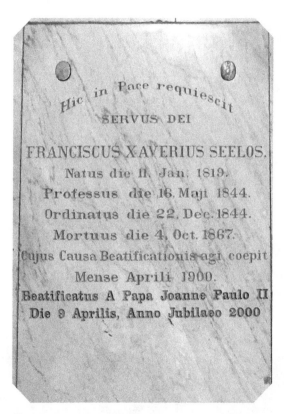

Hic in Pace requiescit
SERVUS DEI

FRANCISCUS XAVERIUS SEELOS.
Natus die 11. Jan. 1819.
Professus die 16. Maji 1844.
Ordinatus die 22. Dec. 1844.
Mortuus die 4. Oct. 1867.
Cujus Causa Beatificationis agi coepit
Mense Aprili 1900.
Beatificatus A Papa Joanne Paulo II
Die 9 Aprilis, Anno Jubilaeo 2000

This carved marble slab marks Fr. Seelos' grave at St. Mary's Assumption Church. His relics are now interred in a reliquary at the National Shrine of Blessed Francis Xavier Seelos in New Orleans.

This portrait of Blessed Francis Xavier Seelos was painted by Giuseppe Antonio Lomuscio, an Italian artist.

Postscript

FR. FRANCIS XAVIER SEELOS passed from earthly life into eternity on October 4, 1867, in the early evening, surrounded by his confreres. Immediately after his death, he was clothed in purple vestments and laid out for visitation in St. Mary's Church. Church bells tolled, informing the faithful of his passing. All night, people came to pray. They prayed for him and to him for his intercession in their needs. They touched books, rosaries, and other articles to his body. They knew he was special, and they wanted his holy presence to somehow continue among them. The solemn funeral Mass was celebrated at eight o'clock on Saturday morning. He was laid to rest at St. Mary's Assumption Church under the statue of Our Mother of Sorrows, which he had blessed on July 17, and where he had prayed as the parish priest. It was reported that his intercession was felt as early as three days after his death, on October 7.

The journey toward the canonization of Fr. Francis Xavier Seelos has been interspersed with long periods of inactivity. The devotion of the faithful has kept his cause alive. It began with Br. Louis Kenning's account of the death of this holy man. He had attended to Fr. Seelos throughout his dying. Two years later he wrote to Rome, urging the Redemptorist authorities to start collecting materials concerning Fr. Seelos for his future canonization. Fr. Seelos' letters were collected by Fr. Bernard Beck in Pittsburgh, and Frs. Joseph Wuest and Joseph Wissel wrote the first Seelos biography. Twenty years after Fr. Seelos' death, Fr. John Berger was charged with writing a more thorough biography. He died before it was completed, but Fr. Peter Zimmer brought it to completion.

In 1898, Fr. Wissel was appointed the first vice postulator of the cause of canonization for Fr. Seelos. From 1900 to 1903, he collected the testimonies of seventy-six witnesses who could attest to Fr. Seelos' virtue. In 1903, Francis Xavier Seelos' body was exhumed and examined. The metal coffin was opened and found to be half-filled with water. Only bones remained. These remains were reinterred in a wooden coffin, sealed by the archbishop of New Orleans, and reburied in the sanctuary of St. Mary's. This new crypt was marked by a carved marble slab.

Beyond, in the beautiful meadows of heaven,
Where the blossoms do not look faded;
Beyond, where everything is budding,
    everything blossoming
And gleams fragrant in the new son of heaven;
Beyond, where the fruits of life are eternally
    ripening
And cold winds do not whistle through leafless
    branches;
Beyond, where God's children play in green
    groves,
And the joyful heart feels the glow of pure love;
Beyond, where a beam of love nourishes now the
    tired heart
And it, now fully satisfied, desires nothing more.
There, yes there alone
Is my pleasure one day to be;
There, where a God loves us,
Nothing clouds our love.
There, where our love will be so pure
And yet will be so full.
There, where a paradise
Will know how to tell us
Everything God has done—
And what he can do—
When he rewards virtue

That then lives in light;
She who once was heavily burdened
Feels herself now fully blessed.
Beyond, in the free land of life,
Where every bond of earth will be loosed;
There, where every child of God is free,
All have become grown up.
Beyond, I will look and enjoy,
And rejoicing, greet those new meadows
That a God forms according to his heart's
    pleasure,
And leads before the eyes of the enraptured
    child—
Not romantically wild
Not in the image of sin!
Everything is great in new dimensions
In the eternally mild spheres of heaven.

The results of Fr. Wissel's research, along with a collection of Blessed Seelos' writings, were sent to the Vatican, where they were examined by the promoter of the faith—then known as the devil's advocate. The investigation concluded there was nothing against the Catholic faith or morality in any of the materials. Further testimonies concerning the holiness of Fr. Seelos' life were gathered in Pittsburgh, Baltimore, New Orleans, and at Augsburg in

Bavaria. These were gathered in 1908 into a *summarium*. Despite this activity, nothing further developed until 1933, when Cardinal Amleto Giovanni Cicognani, then apostolic delegate to the United States, learned of the lives of both Fr. John Neumann and Fr. Francis Xavier Seelos. Cardinal Cicognani wrote to the Redemptorist superior general in Rome, suggesting that more investigation into the lives of these two Redemptorists was warranted. Later, Cardinal Cicognani published the book *Sanctity in America*, which included an account of Fr. Seelos.

Even during the years of silence, devotion continued to flourish among the faithful toward Fr. Seelos. A bulletin promoting Seelos' cause, *Seelos and Sanctity*, began publication in the early 1960s. In 1969, Fr. Michael Curley's biography, *Cheerful Ascetic*, was first published. The devotions seeking the intercession of Fr. Seelos steadily increased.

The Redemptorist postulator in Rome, Fr. Nicola Ferrante, took up the Seelos cause more diligently. In 1983, Bishop Stanley Ott, the bishop of Baton Rouge, Louisiana, inquired into the progress toward canonization. His questioning prompted the appointment of Fr. Carl Hoegerl in 1984 to move the cause further along. Fr. Hoegerl's work was invaluable. In 1994, Archbishop Francis Schulte of New Orleans appointed a commission, including Fr. Hoegerl and two other historians, to prepare a report. It was found that all was in order and nothing was overlooked for the continuation of Fr. Seelos' cause. The Congregation of Saints affirmed the process and gave an affirmative vote for the cause of Fr. Seelos. In 1999, eight theologians gathered to report that Servant of God Francis Xavier Seelos had indeed practiced heroic virtue. By this time, the former postulator in Rome, Fr. Ferrante, had died, and Fr. Antonio Marrazzo was appointed his successor to carry on the process.

In 1966, a woman named Angela Boudreaux learned she had a malignant tumor which had metastasized into 90 percent of her liver. She was given scant hope of recovery. Even so, she prayed for Fr. Seelos' intercession and made a rapid recovery. In 1971, a surgery unrelated to the liver malignancy showed that the liver was normal. On January 5, 2000, the events surrounding Angela's recovery were determined to be miraculous.

With the decree of heroic virtue declared and the acceptance of Angela Boudreaux's cure as a miracle, on January 27, 2000, St. John Paul II promulgated both the heroic virtue of Fr. Seelos and the miracle. He then notified the superior general of the Redemptorists in Rome that Seelos was to be beatified. The date for beatification was set for April 9, 2000, and St. John Paul II declared Fr. Seelos Blessed. October 5, the day after his death in 1867, was to be observed as his feast day.

But for him to be canonized, more work is needed. A second unexplained happening attributed to the intercession of Blessed Seelos must be presented which, in turn, the Vatican could declare a miracle. This is required for a canonization to be declared. The cause for Blessed Seelos' canonization goes on today. In New Orleans, the National Shrine of Blessed Seelos continues to receive a steady flow of pilgrims begging for the intercession of Fr. Seelos in their needs.

Portrait painted by Giuseppe Antonio Lomuscio

A Prayer for Blessed Seelos' Intercession

Let us pray together:

Blessed Seelos, acknowledging our dependence upon almighty God and recognizing the power of your intercession, we come to you because many prayers have been answered through your intercession. As we submit to the will of God in heaven, we pray that our petitions be granted for God's honor and glory and for the salvation of souls.

Blessed Francis Seelos, pray for us.

Blessed Seelos, manifest yourself to all who seek your help. Teach us to prefer God in everything we do. Protect us from spiritual and temporal harm. Many times, you experienced the sorrows of life and yet you overcame those trials. Show us how to overcome our trials and tribulations.

Blessed Francis Seelos, pray for us.

Blessed Seelos, you had great devotion to our eucharistic Lord. Pray that we may know and love the Eucharist as you did. Give strength and courage to the Vicar of Christ. Protect our bishops, priests, and religious. May all be zealous for the kingdom of God. Enlighten the minds of people who seek truth. Protect loved ones away from home. You are familiar with places where we live, work, and pray. As a priest, you lived here among our ancestors. You taught them, blessed them, and prayed for them. Now we come to you. We are confident you will not disappoint us.

Blessed Francis Seelos, pray for us.

Pause now to mention the special intentions of our hearts.

Whatever God grants, we accept with a deep sense of gratitude. We thank him. We praise him. We want to be with him forever.

O my God, we adore your infinite majesty with all the powers of our being. We thank you for the graces and gifts you have bestowed upon your faithful people through the intercession of Blessed Seelos, and ask you to hear our prayers this day. We beseech you to grant us the favors which we humbly ask of your fatherly mercy.

We have come here to venerate one of the great blesseds of God. As Blessed Francis Seelos adds his prayers to ours, may our needs be met in the mercy of God, and may our petitions be heard. Amen.

A present-day view of the National Shrine of Blessed Francis Xavier Seelos

For Further Reading

Burkey, Blaine, OFM Cap. *Seelos: The Cumberland Years*. Seelos Center, New Orleans, 2010. Seelos.org.

Curley, Michael J., CSsR. *Cheerful Ascetic*. Seelos Center, New Orleans, 2002. Seelos.org.

Hoegerl, Carl, CSsR, and Von Stamwitz, Alicia. *A Life of Blessed Francis Xavier Seelos*. Liguori Publications; Liguori, Missouri; 2000. Liguori.org.

Hoegerl, Carl, CSsR. *Sincerely, Seelos: The Collected Letters of Blessed Francis Xavier Seelos*. Seelos Center, New Orleans, 2008. Seelos.org.

Hoegerl, Carl, CSsR. *With All Gentleness: A Life of Blessed Francis Xavier Seelos, CSsR*. Seelos Center, New Orleans, 2018. Seelos.org.

Miller, Byron, CSsR, editor. *Death, Where Is Your Sting?* Seelos Center, New Orleans, 2006. Seelos.org.

For Further Reading

About the Author

Fr. Richard Boever, CSsR, PhD, has been in the Catholic ministry since 1974. He served as a parish priest and pastor in St. Louis and Chicago, taught theology at Newman University and Saint Louis University, served as a university chaplain, and he has been the director of Redemptorist formation for the prenovitiate program. He also held various positions at Liguori Publications, including president and publisher. He was a retreat director in Oconomowoc, Wisconsin, and served as a research expert at the Neumann Shrine in Philadelphia. Fr. Rich currently is the executive director at the National Shrine of Blessed Francis Xavier Seelos in New Orleans. He has authored many books for Liguori Publications, including *Saint John Neumann: His Writings and Spirituality* (2010) and *The 5W's of the Catholic Faith: Living in Hope* (2012).

The National Shrine of Blessed Francis Xavier Seelos, CSsR, was established by the Redemptorist Fathers and Brothers in 1959 as a practical result of renewed interest in the cause of Fr. Seelos in Rome. The mission and goal of the shrine is to promote the canonization cause of Fr. Seelos through vital ministry carried on in his name.

The shrine is located in St. Mary's Assumption Church in New Orleans and features the remains of Fr. Seelos, his original lead coffin, artifacts from his life, and first-class relics of various saints. Inside the reliquary room, a prayer partner— along with a Seelos relic crucifix—is available to pray with you and for your special intentions.

**The National Shrine
of Blessed Francis Xavier Seelos, CSsR**
919 Josephine Street
New Orleans, Louisiana 70130, USA
(504) 525-2495
Seelos.org